RECENT IMAGES OF JESUS CHRIST PROVE HIS DIVINITY

BY Adelaide Mary Abraham

AuthorHouse™
1663 Liberty Drive
Bloomington, IN 47403
www.authorhouse.com
Phone: 1-800-839-8640

Published by AuthorHouse 03/08/2013

ISBN: 978-1-4685-4142-7 (sc)

authorHOUSE®

DEDICATED to the MOST PRECIOUS BLOOD of

Our Lord and Saviour Jesus Christ

GYE NYAME

(Only God would make such wonders possible)

"With God all things are possible"

Mark 10:17-30

This book was compiled by Adelaide Mary Abraham.

Many thanks to Rev. Father Leo who edited this book at very short notice.

DECEMBER 2007

The birth of Jesus is depicted here, not in a stable, but in a woods. It is a thought-provoking picture. Christ said, "Whoever receives one such child in my name receives me." (Mt. 18.5)

I pray for the grace of empathy, the wisdom to recognize the Christ Child today, born in a tenement, a barrio, a suburb. Help me, Lord, to carry the spirit of this joyous feast throughout the new year. Let me celebrate the coming of Christ every day. Let me welcome him wherever I find him. May I always rejoice: Hallelujah, Jesus Christ is born!

"ADORATION IN THE WOODS"
Fillipo Lippi c. 1406-1469

Jesus Christ our Saviour has put together a few of His miraculous pictures to prove that He was God all along though He put on a human nature, "And the Word was made Flesh and dwelt amongst us, full of grace and truth; we have beheld his glory, glory as of the only Son from God."

Jesus Christ is very much alive. Alleluia!

After Our Lord's resurrection before he ascended into heaven, he summoned his disciples to meet him on the mountain. When the disciples saw Him they fell down before Him. Jesus came up to them and said, "All authority in heaven and on earth has been given to me. Go, therefore, and make disciples of all nations; baptize them in the name of the Father and of the Son and of the Holy Spirit, and teach them to observe all the commands I have given you. And know that I am with you always; <u>yes</u>, even to the end of time."

1

Just as Jesus says He is one with the Father I think I can also say the same of the Heavenly Father; I used to walk hand in hand with God Our Father and I used to call Him "Sweetie Pie." Our Lord and I share the same sentiment. I have always said from my early childhood that Our Lord and I are one because God wills it so. Our pictures testify to that. A few hours after I wrote down my relationship with God Our Father and Jesus it was time to go to Church, so I went to Mass, which was Christmas Day.

I had taken a small booklet entitled <u>God Manifest in the Flesh</u> with me. I opened page 5 during Mass because that was the page I opened at home before I left but did not have time to read since I was running late. As I opened the page, Rev. Father Leo in his preaching said, "No one has ever seen God. The only Son, God, who is at the Father's side, has revealed him; and also anyone to whom the Father has revealed Him." John 1:18. Rev. Father Leo was referring to the Gospel for that clay which was Christmas Day; and to my amazement, the page I opened during the preaching was saying the same thing as Rev. Fr. Leo only our Gospel was offering a shorter version. The booklet however; was offering a complete version and it went on to say what we all know concerning this matter and that is: Because of the Lord's frequent mentioning of His Father, Philip said, "Show us the Father and it sufficeth us." John 1:18. Jesus answered, "Have I been so long time with you and yet hast thou not known me, Philip? He that has seen Me has seen the Father and how sayest thou then show us the Father?" Believest thou not that I am in the Father, and the Father in me? The words that I speak unto you I do not speak on my own authority; but the Father who dwells in me does his work. Believe me that I am in the Father and the Father in me; or else believe me for the sake of the works themselves. Truly, truly, I say to you, he who believes in me will also do the works that I do; and greater works than these will he do, because I go to the Father. Whatever you ask in my name, I will do it, that the Father may be glorified in the Son; if you ask anything in my name, I will do it.

"If you love me, you will keep my commands. And I will pray the Father, and he will give you another Counselor, to be with you forever, even the Spirit of truth, whom the world cannot receive because it neither sees him nor knows him; you know him for he dwells with you, and will be in you.

I will not leave you desolate; I will come to you. Yet a little while, the world will see me no more, but you will see me;. because I live, you will live also. In that day you will know that I am in the Father, and you in me, and I in you. He who has my commandments and keeps them, he it is who loves me; and he who loves me will be loved by my Father, and I will love him and manifest myself to him." John 1:9-22. I asked the same question one of the Apostles asked Jesus, namely, "Lord, how is it that you manifest yourself to me and not to the world?" Jesus' answer was, "If a man loves me, he will keep my word, and my Father will love him, and we will come to him, and make our home with him." You may still say you do not understand how we can see the Father in the Son. We can see the Father in the Son just as we can say to a man, "I can see your father in you because you are so much like him." We cannot however, say that Jesus is the Father just as we cannot say that a human son is his father. Jesus and the Father are one in the Blessed Trinity, the one Godhead, but the Persons in the Trinity are always distinct, explains Rev. Father Leo. Right after Mass in church, a friend gave me a Christmas card which showed the Lion of Judah lying with the Lamb of God. For the first time, I felt the power and the awesomeness of the work Our Lord had commissioned me to do. I do not remember seeing any Christmas card depicting an image from the old Testament. I asked Fr. Leo about the reference to the Lamb of God and the Lion of Judah. Rev. Fr. Leo told me Jesus, the Lamb of God, is also the Lion of Judah. He also said that the "Lamb of God and Lion of Judah are powerful titles especially Lamb of God, but they are metaphorical titles, not literal titles. He added that, "Metaphorical titles can strike us more forcefully than literal descriptions." He also said that putting the lamb and the lion together is a good way of describing God's power and God's sacrificial love "even more powerful for us than the proper names of divine persons would be although the proper names are far more important."

At the same time, I saw a book in front of me, and out of wonder I opened the book and to my amazement, I saw one of my cuttings from Most Holy Redeemer. The following is what Bishop Donald F. Hanchon, Pastor of Most Holy Redeemer says about the Trinity:

"We know God as Trinity because of Jesus, who prayed to God as Father, called himself "one with the Father," "the only Son of God" — and promised to send us "another Advocate," the Holy Spirit which joined him to the Father." There is more but this serves my purpose of writing for now and that is to prove my relationship with the Holy Trinity.

Listen to this, I was going to end up here. I saw a book entitled <u>God Calling</u>. I opened the book and I saw my picture stuck in that page — guess what the page is saying, "My Father and I are One." I thought Jesus must be talking. In that same page was a bright yellow paper shaped like a big Key with the name Jesus. Naturally, I turned to the back of the key and I noticed I had written, "The Father and I are one." And I had added, " Yes, Father and Lord, and Holy Spirit."

Two days after Rev. Fr. Leo and I were talking about the Lamb of God and the Lion of Judah because of the reference made concerning these titles in the Christmas card that I said a friend gave me, I walked into Saturday evening Mass and to my amazement, our same Rev. Fr. Leo was preaching about the Lamb of God because it was the Gospel for that week-end, which was really amazing. Even our Sunday Bulletin remarked that it was too soon for the Gospel to be hinting at Lent, which is months away, so close to Christmas. In fact, when I was referring to the message in the Christmas card my friend gave me, I deleted the reference to the Lamb of God and the Lion of Judah because I said we are still somewhat in the Christmas Season only to find out according to Our Lord we should not lose sight of Lent even during Christmas. Remember His preaching during Advent about His Second coming warning us all to be prepared? He said, "As it was in the days of Noah, so it will be at the coming of the Son of Man." (Mt.24:27) He admonishes us to stay awake. For we do not know on which day the Lord will come. Advent and Lent are the two special seasons that the Catholic Church has set aside to give us Catholics the opportunity to examine our lives and to make the necessary penance while we strive to live a better and holy life. We should focus our attention on Christ who instructs us to live the <u>Beatitudes </u>in conjunction with the <u>Ten Commandments</u> if we are to attain eternal life.

John the Baptist's preaching was the same, "Prepare ye the way of the Lord. Make straight His path. For the Kingdom of God is at hand,"(Mt. 3:2-3) implying now, and John focuses his attention on the Lamb of God who has come to direct us to that Kingdom.

The Church Bulletin I picked up from Church that Saturday Evening Mass talked solely about Jesus as "the Lamb who was led to slaughter." (Is. 53-7) The Bulletin continues, "And even though our celebration of Easter is months away, already the Gospel sounds the theme of the direction in which we are heading." It continues to say,"We hear John the Baptist describe Jesus as the Lamb of God in today's Gospel. We use that same imagery when we plead with the Lamb of God in the litany that we sing at Mass during the breaking of the bread."

In the First Reading, it is mentioned that "in the Book of Exodus, it is the Lamb of God whose blood marks the way for the angel of death to pass over the places where the blood is seen." Adding that, "as Lamb of God, Jesus shed his blood, marking all who are baptized in his name with the Holy Spirit, which John the Baptist describes in today's Gospel. The Gospel emphasizes that, "Sin and death have no power over us because we are saved by the blood of the Lamb." Jesus is the new Paschal Lamb, and we are saved through the shedding of His blood and this symbolizes our victory over death through Christ, explains Father Thomas, Pastor of St. Anne Catholic Church. The reference to the Lamb of God on the Christmas card I deleted from my writing was the Gospel for that Sunday.

I actually threw away the Christmas card my friend gave me to my regret, because I did not like the animal imagery. Besides, I thought we were still not quite done with the Easter celebration. When I realized what the Lord was doing, I asked my friend for another Christmas card, and luckily, she had an extra one of the same card with the lion lying with the lamb motif. I was amazed she had another one. This was in May when all this happened. Now, see how Christ proves Himself.

On September 4th, 2011, I met Rev. Michael Jones, a pastor in the elevator. He was just leaving the building after visiting a lady friend of mine who had raised him when he was seven or nine years old. I had been visiting his mother every Sunday after church and we will say a little prayer together especially The Our Father. The pastor and I were talking about the changing weather. I then showed him a book I had written entitled *Divine Intimacy with my Saviour*. I was rushing to show my book to friends at a meeting after church. When I learned he was my friend's son and a pastor, I gave him one of my books, and he also gave me a beautiful new poetry book he had just written entitled *Poetry Inspired by the Lion of Judah* the very same topic I had written about in my second book entitled' <u>Recent Images of Jesus Christ Prove His Divinity</u>. And to my amazement, he had a picture of the Lion lying with the Lamb at the back of his poetry book just like my Christmas card. The imagery on the back of Pastor Michael Jones' poetry book was the same imagery on the Christmas card my friend gave me. And to prove Himself further, Jesus reiterates His message.

— *Peace on Earth* Statue

Based on Isaiah 11:6, this beautiful statue
depicts natural enemies lying at peace together.

    I saw a small Religious magazine lying on my table; I opened it at random — what

did I see but the same imagery from the Prophet (Isaiah 11: 6) depicting natural enemies lying

together in peace. It was a statue and below it read: PEACE ON EARTH. A few days later I

visited my sister in Canada. Whilst there, she ran out from her garden calling out in a cautious

low tone saying, "Come and see, come and see." When I went, I saw a squirrel surrounded by

six or eight little birdies eating happily together.

As I said earlier, I threw away the part of the animal imagery from the Christmas card a friend gave me but kept the part that reads ,

"...and on earth peace, good will toward men (Luke 2:14)." Immediately, the thought of the full message came to me and when I opened up a book *The Mystical City of God*, abridged by Mary of Agreda, I went straight to the passage that reads, "suddenly appeared a great multitude of celestial army who in voices of sweet harmony sang to the Most High these words, 'Glory to God in the highest and on earth peace to men of good will.'" As the angels were found "rehearsing this divine canticle, so new to the world, they disappeared to heaven."

The *Mystical City of God* had more to say about the shepherds. The angel Gabriel told the shepherds they were specially blessed not because they had accepted their meager state in life that had been allotted them by God, but because of their humility and their poverty as well as their being despised by the world. Also, they are favored because of their constant search like their fellow Israelites who await sincerely for the coming of the Messiah. Our Lord sees the shepherds as Himself, free from the corrupt practices and arrogance of this world. "They exhibited in the circumstances of their calling the office, which the good Shepherd had come to fulfill in knowing His sheep and being known to them. Hence they merited to be called and invited, as the first fruits of the Saints by the Savior Himself, to be the very first ones, to whom the eternal and incarnate Word manifested Himself and by whom He wished to be praised, served, and adored. Hence the angel Gabriel was sent to them as they were watching their flock in human form and in great splendor."

8

I remembered at once a great nativity picture bearing the picture of all three persons of the Holy Trinity that had been sitting on top of the printer which I hid in my closet just before I went out of town. I rushed quickly to my bed room and headed towards my closet but I was met with a new beautiful bag at the side entrance of my closet. I yelled out, "No, this can't be the Holy Trinity. The bag is beautiful alright but I would not sit my Holy picture on the floor though the bag is beautiful and new and all that." As I lamented, I said, "Oh no, it cannot be;" but I was happy I found the picture so quickly. I looked into the bag and I saw my Nativity picture wrapped up in a new beautiful cloth as I always do. And I saw next to it my small cutting from the Michigan Catholic with the angelic message also in Latin everywhere, which read "Gloria in Excelsis Deo, et in terra pax hominibus, bonae volumtatis" I had already seen the Latin version twice. Meanwhile, I had to run to the store for a cartridge for the computer. When I got to the store, I was thinking about the Latin version and the letter 'c' in the word Excelsis. I opened my note book to look for the number for the cartridge and there it was again next to some notes I had written about the Messiah, Our crucified Saviour. It was both in English and in Latin.

When I was making the cutting through the Michigan Catholic (Sunday Catholic Publication) I had cut through the message because when I was making the cutting I was aiming at a Nativity display on the back. I did not know there was the angelic message in the front bearing a bright Star and with the message in big bold letters saying, "Glory to God in- etc". The full song to the Most High is -

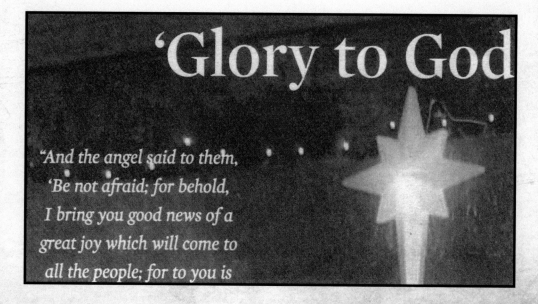

"Glory to God

"And the angel said to them,
'Be not afraid; for behold,
I bring you good news of a
great joy which will come to
all the people; for to you is

"Glory to God in the highest and on earth peace to men of good will."

"And suddenly there was

with the angel a multitude

of heavenly host

praising God and saying

Glory to God in the highest,

and on earth peace to men

of good will."

Almighty God Himself wants the whole world to know He did not send His only begotten Son for commercial and frivolous reasons or for an occasion for the world to have a pastime. This is the occasion that demands the highest respect to say the least. It calls for the highest contemplation in prayer and sacrifice. We should worry about the angels' message; it is not to everyone that the angels greeted with peace. In one of the Christmas miraculous pictures Jesus was crying on Christmas Day even with His royal crown on His head on the altar as a woman who must be His mother, tries to cheer Him up. We should be thankful to Our Heavenly Father, "FOR GOD SO LOVED THE WORLD, THAT HE GAVE HIS ONLY BEGOTTEN SON, THAT WHOEVER BELIEVES IN HIM SHOULD NOT PERISH BUT HAVE ETERNAL LIFE. FOR GOD SENT HIS SON INTO THE WORLD, NOT TO CONDEMN THE WORLD BUT THAT THE WORLD MIGHT BE SAVED THROUGH HIM." I felt very happy I found my Nativity picture with the Holy Trinity so quickly.

God so loved the world that
He gave His only Son.

John 3:16

It has always been like this throughout the writing. I will be looking for something and it is as if the Good Lord is handing it to me. When I found my picture by my closet I said to Heavenly Father, "How did you get here?"

How time flies, — today November 3rd, almost a year ago, I was looking for something for somebody , and I saw that little piece I tore from the Christmas card I said a friend gave me after Mass depicting an image from the old Testament. St. Luke's words which I just quoted about 'Peace on Earth' give the same message as Prophet Isaiah's imagery, and I quote, "The wolf shall dwell with the lamb, and the leopard shall lie down with the kid, and the calf and the lion and the fatling together, and a little child shall lead them. The cow and the bear shall feed; their young shall lie down together; and the lion shall eat straw like the ox (Is 11:6-7).

The utopian imagery depicted in the Christmas card with reference to the wolf lying with the lamb is also mentioned by Prophet Isaiah in the reading for the First Sunday of Advent.

The prophet says, "A shoot shall sprout from the stump of Jesse, [the Davidic branch], and from its roots a bud shall blossom" (Is 11:1) with the coming of a new king. This new king will prosper and will be inspired with wisdom and strength. He will be a just judge and give the poor their due. He will restore paradise itself, a utopian idea which Isaiah expresses in the beautiful imagery such as the one depicted in the Christmas card, namely, the wolf lying with the lamb, and the calf and the young lying together bringing about such peace and harmony as have not been realized since Adam's disobedience. Isaiah's lyrical prophesy is fulfilled in Christ. Isaiah based his prophesy on God's message when God sent the Angel Gabriel to Mary to announce the Saviour's birth. In Luke Chapter (1: 26 -33), an angel Gabriel was sent from God to a city of Galilee called Nazareth, to a virgin betrothed to a man whose name was Joseph, of the house of David. And the angel said to her, "Behold, you will conceive in your womb and bear a son, and you shall call his name Jesus. He will be great, and will be called the son of the Most High; and the Lord God will give to him the throne of his father David, and will reign over the house of Jacob for ever; and of his kingdom there will be no end."

According to Isaiah, when Noah sent out a dove a second time from the Ark to see if the water had receded, the dove did not bring a simple olive branch, but instead brought the root of Jesse which is in the person of Jesus Christ. In the Acts of the Apostles 13:22-26, Paul said, that God made David the king of our ancestors, of whom he approved in these words, "I have selected David son of Jesse, a man after my own heart who will carry out my purpose. " To keep his promise, God has raised up for Israel one of David's descendants, Jesus, as Saviour whose coming was heralded by John the Baptist when he proclaimed a baptism of repentance.

When I was in the primary school, we took turns every morning in the Religious Class to read the Three Synoptic Gospels, which are full of the miracles that Christ performed here on earth during His public Ministry. It was our First Lesson for the day.

I felt so elated with the readings so I said to Our Lord one morning during our Religious Class, "Let us some day show the world who you really are;" hence these numerous miraculous pictures.

I do not think Christ has ever left this earth. It is true that He ascended to His Father after His resurrection but from my experience I have never missed His presence here on earth. I have known Him intimately since my childhood. I have pictured Him by my side everyday. To quote a few lines from William Wordsworth's Ode To Immortality — Intimations of Early Childhood:

"But trailing clouds of glory do we come

From God, who is our home:

Heaven lies about us in our infancy"

This quotation in my mind could mean an awareness or perception of things of heaven in our world.

The Light of the soul, which we inherit, transforms or glorifies all that we see. This Light is the "Light of Christ." We Catholics celebrate Advent every year in preparation for the birth of Christ. Advent therefore means "the coming or arrival" and here it refers to the four weeks season of preparation for the coming of Our Lord on Christmas Day. "THE WORD WAS MADE FLESH AND DWELT AMONGST US. (John 1:14)."

Jesus, "The Light of The World"

In Him was life; and the life was the "light" of men. There was a man sent from God, whose name was John. The same came for a witness, to bear witness of the Light that all men through him might believe. He was not the Light, but was sent to bear witness of that Light. "That was the true Light which lighteth every man that cometh into the world." John 1:3.6-9.

The significance of the Light we have received in *Baptism is the Light of Christ*; through *Baptism we have union with God*. The Church advises us to rejoice reminding us about *our*

13

immortality in Christ, the Light of the world. I visited my sister in Canada. I had left a few items such as Holy pictures and photos I got from Immaculate Heart of Mary Church. I went back for those Holy pictures. The largest among them was a picture of Jesus standing erect, looking rather stem, to me. I love that picture very much so when I brought it home, I took it to where I was typing still admiring it as usual - the way He was dressed etc. but I did not think very much about what the picture really meant until I brought it to my studio, shall I say. Then I brought it closer to where I was typing, and I said to myself; "Let me look at the title. I don't believe I have not looked at it all this time". Then I looked, and it read, "Jesus The Light of The World". I then said to myself, "This is what I am typing: Jesus as The Light of The World." I reached for the picture again to have another look and I became even more excited. I looked at the Lord's Face and my joy was full, for the following reason: a few years ago, on the Feast of Christ The King something extraordinary happened to me at Corpus Christi.

As a Eucharistic Minister, I took the Communion bowl and the platter to the Sacristy for a final wash. When I took the first platter to wash there was a small communion and another communion shaped like a chalice so I consumed them. The same thing happened when I took the second platter or bowl so I consumed them as well. Now, the Lord's Face on the aforesaid picture is the story here. The picture of Christ as The Light of the World has on His cheek the shape of a chalice and on His forehead the shape of Holy Communion. I had four pictures that bore the same description. Before I found the picture 'Jesus The Light of World,' I looked for my four pictures but did not find them. I remember saying the Good Lord would rather I share so I thought of wrapping three intending to give them away and keeping one. I think I must have given all four away and leaving none for myself. Now I have one picture 'Jesus The Light of The World 'with two messages combined.

Jesus showed me something else. On Maundy or Holy Thursday of this year which was 21ˢᵗ of April, 2011, I found my glasses that have been missing for months at the entrance of the altar of repose where the Eucharist is kept on Holy Thursday, two days before Easter. And at the entrance was exactly the same picture I said I had with Christ's forehead bearing the shape of Holy Communion and His cheek bearing the shape of a chalice. This is how the Good Lord works.

St. Paul reminds us that if we die in Baptism with the Lord, we shall rise with Him in His resurrection.

The following is a hymn we sing at church in line with what I have written.

Keep in mind that Jesus Christ has died for us

and is risen from the dead, He is our saving

Lord, He is joy for all ages.

If you die with the Lord, you shall rise with the Lord.

St. Paul also says "I no longer live but Christ lives in me (Gal.2:20)", and in II Cor. 4:10), he says, "We carry in our body the dying of Jesus, so that the life of Jesus also may be manifested in our body."

I thought I was done with the story about "Christ The Light of the World" but apparently it was not so with the Lord. I went to my room lifted some boxes looking for something; I heard a pamphlet fall —I reached for it. I saw at the very top in big bold writing, "CHRIST IS VICTOR." There were two sub-titles; the one on the left reads, "A Glimpse of Heaven," and the one on the right reads in very dark print the word "LIGHT." Let's talk about the "light" since my main subject is "Jesus The Light of The World." The following is what the author, Pastor Joshua Daniel says and I quote,

A matter of grave concern has been heavy on my heart.

Why are we not exalting the name of Jesus Christ,

unable to set up such a flood of _light_ around us that

men and women readily recognize that Jesus is

the _author of light_ Jesus is the Sun of Righteousness,

and is the Light of the world?

The pastor goes on to say,

There should be a clamouring

around us saying, "Give us that light." The world should

be looking at us and saying, "We need the light which is in you."

Pastor Daniel asks the question, "Why is it that we are unable to arrest that normal attention that light automatically begets?" He adds that, "Even the creatures of darkness seem somehow to draw near to light rather timorously it might seem" He saw a bird on the ground late at night slowly crawling towards light that emanated from his tent. etc. He says that, the normal tendency or reaction of a creature should be to turn away from the light and to look for a dark corner but these creatures of darkness rather advance towards the light. This leads him to wonder, "Why should we say we are Christians? Why should we say we are those that walk in the light, as He is in the light? Our Lord has no darkness at all. There is no darkness in Him, we are told."

Pastor Joshua Daniel asks, "Why is our light not shining in the prevailing gloom of our day, which to him is a matter of great sorrow?" He believes there are some causes for this lack of light. His first reason is the lack of faith in prayer. He goes on to say, "When a person who says he is a Christian does not require the breath of faith you can be sure he is as dead as a door nail." He complains that, "This talk of being a Christian without adequate prayer. which begets light, example or blessing, cannot any longer pass unchallenged." Talking about good example, I went to the kitchen for something and I saw the following on the back of a letter I received from Solanus Casey Center: "If we're not giving our youth the role models of faith and holiness they need, where will they turn?" On the front of the envelope, it reads: "Then God intervened to write the life story every young American should hear..." Now to go back to "Jesus The Light of the World" where we left off reiterating Our Lord having no darkness in Him. That in Him, "There is no darkness at all." At this juncture, I went to the next room and it was as if the

Lord handed me a beautiful blue pad I received from the Salesian Missions. The pad had a Mission on a hill with a tall beacon; had a handsome face, and a blue hat holding, a Big Light, and it reads,

"God is light and in Him is no darkness at all" -I John 1:5.

Two weeks before Christmas of 2011, as I was compiling my notes on Jesus The Light of the world, I received a powerful letter from Rev. Fr. Kevin Nadolski, Director of Development who resides at a place called Childs, Maryland -

A BIG CHRISTMAS STAR

shines in the blue sky.

"This special gift of Jesus

is the grace which helps us to attain what

would otherwise be impossible for us:

The joy and happiness of glory!"

-St. Francis de Sales

Christmas Eve homily, 1613

A Big Christmas Star shines in the beautiful blue sky as you can see with a powerful message from St. Francis de Sales, who lived in the seventeen century. St. Francis de Sales features prominently in my first book entitled *Divine Intimacy with My Saviour.*

Fr. Kevin clearly states the concerns of the poor especially in these difficult times. He adds, "Yet, into this darkness, the light of Jesus shines." He quotes again from St. Francis de Sales' homily, "In the darkness of the night, Our Lord was born and appeared to us an infant lying in a manger. Of course, the mystery is not really dark at all, for God is only light!"

Fr. Kevin says because of our Christian faith, "despite the darkness of the world and our lives, the light of Christ can shine brightly to bring healing, some sense of peace, and ultimately joy and happiness-even when it seems unlikely or impossible!"

The Rev. Father explains that the Ministry of Oblates of Francis de Sales is a community of priests and brothers who minister throughout the world to inspire others to live Jesus, the motto of their patron St. Francis de Sales. And, this is my motto too, to live Jesus. Isn't this amazing, I grew up in St. Francis de Sales parish and I did not even remember the name of this parish until only recently. Little did I know I had something in common with this holy man.

April 29, 2012 was the Fourth Sunday of Easter. And the Gospel was about Christ as the Good Shepherd who lays down his life for His sheep. He enjoys His relationship with the shepherds. Throughout the week I had set up my table to reflect the Gospel message. First, I had a picture of the born babe being led by the Star following the Angel Gabriel's announcement. The Christmas card was set against a miraculous picture of the Risen Lord. Then I had an envelope with the picture of Christ as Shepherd holding His staff and caressing a sheep. The message of the Star reads thus: "WISDOM STILL LEADS THE HEART THAT BELIEVES! And in the inside, "'Whoever believes in the Son has eternal life, he who does not believe in the Son has no life. '" John 3:36. The next thing I had was an envelope I had addressed to myself thus: "THE GOOD SHEPHERD with The Lord's Picture (Holy of Holies) to His Blessed Daughter; wishing her A Happy Easter. I had also an Easter card from my Salesian friends wishing me Big Easter Blessings with Our Lord's picture holding His staff and caressing His sheep. I always remember my sister, Regina's interesting story, too about the Good Shepherd; what she saw at her young age. She says that when herself and her four friends were playing in the convent court yard, she thought someone was taking a movie in the sky because she saw a man with his staff upon his shoulder and many sheep following him. She also saw a mother carrying a baby, and some men carrying heavy books. Her other friends saw them, too.

Then off to morning Mass at Most Holy Trinity Church. As I took my seat, I noticed someone had placed that Sunday's brochure called, "The Shepherd's Voice" at where I chose to sit; so I knew it was the Sunday for the Good Shepherd. When the lectrice read the Gospel I read alongside with her though I did not voice it out. I knew the reading so well because I had read it very carefully and had noted what The Good Lord had said painfully about His death, especially when He said, "I lay down my life, that I may take it up again. No one takes it from me, but I lay it down of my own accord. I have power to lay it down and I have power to take it again. I almost clapped my hands for this beautiful speech realizing the Lord has got all the power in His hands. If it were not a sad story I would have applauded. Still, I was happy for Our Great Redeemer that no one had forced Him into anything; and that, He had done what He did simply for the love of mankind and out of His own free will. Jesus added, "This charge I have received from my Father." I have read this passage before. As I was reading it I told Our Lord, "Why don't they read this part of this message in Church? When I said that I immediately saw this same passage in the Shepherd's Voice brochure lying next to the Bible I was reading from. I was amazed because it was the first time I had seen that part in the brochure, though I had read it from the Bible before and had even made notes. I realized I have to pay more attention.

Just as I was about to type, "I am the Good Shepherd; I know mine and mine know me," I felt like resting a little. My Saviour and I sometimes confer on matters. I knew there was a very important message the Lord had pointed out for me to record. I said to my Lord, "Yes Lord, I know." I told Him, I was going up for a minute and as soon as I got back I would definitely record the message for the world. The passage was the very core of last Sunday's Gospel, and I know how important it is to Our Lord. I also love to say it out loud to myself every now and then. And furthermore, what I really love most of all is the name of the Most Holy Trinity brochure, 'The Shepherd's Voice.' I added, it is indeed the Shepherd's Voice and very appropriate, too. I know there is a very important message that should go with all my writing for the Lord and that is, "I am the resurrection and the Life" which Jesus loves so much to talk about. I have been displaying the passage on my window ever since I started writing. Though I knew it by heart, I made an attempt in a hurry to reach for the one by my door which was closer fearing Our Lord would beat me to it and shuffle one into my hands as He usually does. I said Our Lord has spoilt me by always putting the work directly into my hands or making my eye zeroed in on whatever is next for me to write. So, I dashed quickly to my door, I mean quickly before Jesus does it first (I wanted to make an effort to do something, too). Hurrying into my seat, I saw a piece of paper jutting out from a pile of Eucharistic notes (I will be handling next) which reads, "I saw the face of Jesus on the Eucharistic Bread in the Shepherd's Voice brochure from Most Holy Trinity Church with notes on the resurrection and the Eucharist. And, here is the passage again about "The Good Shepherd." The good shepherd lays down his life for his sheep. He who is a hireling and not a shepherd, whose own the sheep are not, sees the wolf coming and leaves the sheep and flees; and the wolf snatches them and scatters them. He flees because he is a hireling and cares nothing for the sheep. "I am the good shepherd, I know mine and mine know me, as the Father knows me and I know the Father, and I lay down my life for my sheep". And I had other sheep, that are not of this fold: I must bring them also, and they will heed my voice. So there shall be one flock, one shepherd." Jesus says to the Jews again,

"Truly, truly, I say to you, I am the door of the sheep. All who came before me are thieves and robbers; but the sheep did not heed them. He says again, truly, truly, I say to you, he who does not enter the sheepfold by the door but climbs in another way, that man is a thief and a robber, but he who enters by the door is the shepherd of the sheep. To him the gatekeeper opens; the sheep hears his voice, and he calls his own sheep by name and leads them out. When he has brought out all his own, he goes before them and the sheep follow him, for they know his voice. A stranger they will not follow, but they will flee from him, for they do not know the voice of strangers." Again, Jesus continues, "I am the door of the sheep; if any man enters by me, he will be saved, and go in and out and find pasture.

The thief comes only to steal and destroy; I came that you may have life, and have it more abundantly. It was the Feast of the Ascension of Jesus into heaven which the Catholic Church celebrates forty days after Our Lord's Resurrection. I had gone up to visit somebody so I asked him what he read that morning from the Bible. He told me he read the passage about Our Shepherd's Voice with reference to Jesus as "The Good Shepherd." I yelled out "What?", because I had just been telling Our Lord how I love this title on the Most Holy Trinity brochure which also bears the name "The Shepherd's Voice." I told Our Lord it was very noble of the Church to come up with such an awesome title; then, I quickly realized myself with the Lord's help that the title must have been taken from the Bible. And truly enough when I told my friend about The Shepherd's Voice brochure, he showed me what he was reading and even gave me a smaller version in a pamphlet from the Bible. The pamphlet that a friend gave me namely, Our Shepherd's Voice also has at the very first line: "My sheep hear my voice, and I know them, and they follow me (John 10:27)". The song that goes with the message reads: "PEACE, PERFECT PEACE."

Now, here 's the message:

It starts by saying, "The Middle East is the cradle of civilization, the area of the world where shepherding was first practiced as a vocation, " adding that, there are still many shepherds there today, practicing their trade even where violent unrest often breaks out. I am recording the story of a Missionary Ron Jones, who serves with the Christian and Missionary Alliance in Israel. He tells his story in a letter.

He said a friend shared with them something she observed "that was a delightful reminder of God's care for us," as she watched a shepherd caring for his flock near an area where guns are fired. She said that "every time the shots rang out, the sheep scattered in fright." The shepherd calmed his sheep by touching each of the sheep with his staff and by speaking calmly to them and the sheep settled down immediately, because they trusted their master. As often as the shots rang out "the same routine unfolded again." The shepherd touched and spoke to his sheep to reassure them that they were safe.

The lesson of this story from the writer is, "If natural shepherds can calm sheep startled by gunfire, what can our heavenly shepherd do?" He continues, "In fact, Judaism and the Roman Empire together never could drown out the reassuring voice of Jesus. This same voice not only calls but also calms."

I then stood up wondering what to write next or how to write all that I was viewing because a lot of good things were coming from different directions. Again I stood up, this time in front of my round glass table viewing all the lovely miraculous pictures that were there before me. There was also a card with Prayer Request from the Salesian Missions with The 23 Psalm

THE LORD IS MY SHEPHERD I SHALL NOT WANT

I was also thinking about the beautiful tapestry of the Good Shepherd in church and the things I heard at Mass,.and seeing the beauty of Father's world with His saints in spite of all the bad things that are happening; they are nothing compared with God's grandeur; and so I knew I was ready to write even more. For those who are suffering, listen to what Paul says, "The sufferings of this present time are not worthy to be compared with the glory which shall be revealed in us Romans 8:18." The Gospel for the Fourth Sunday of Easter says it all for which we rejoice, "See what love the Father has given us, that we should be called children of God; and so we are. The reason why the world does not know us is that it did not know him. Beloved, we are God's children now, it does not yet appear what we shall be, but we know that when he appears, we shall be like him, for we shall see him as he is. AND EVERYONE WHO HOPES IN HIM PURIFIES HIMSELF AS HE IS PURE" (1 John 3:1-2).

Throughout the writing, I kept receiving letters from the Salesian Missions asking for donations to feed the orphanage etc. I did not make anything out of it except that I remembered Our Lord introducing St. Bosco to me during the Exhibition of the Holy Shroud in Santa Cruz which made me attended his Feast Day Masses since then. Suddenly, I realized something. The letters that came from the Salesian Missions ask the following question, "Who are the Salesians? Their answer is amazing and very interesting. Listen to this:

In 1859, a young priest named John Bosco and eighteen young men who were once street children he cared for began a new society. John Bosco called them the Salesians after St. Francis de Sales, Bishop of Geneva, whom he had always admired for his kindness and religious zeal.

A new era in caring for young people had begun. If you have read my book *Divine Intimacy with My Saviour,* you will recall that St. Francis de Sales features prominently in my book. It is this same St. Francis de Sales of whom it is said, "It pleased Our Lord to give a signal manifestation of His love for His chosen servant. The face of the saint while preaching became transfigured, shining with heavenly light, while burning words fell from his lips, touching even the hardest hearts, all recognized even in his own country the Seer and the Prophet."

Today with Priests, Brothers, Sisters numbering more than 34,000—the Salesians; feed, clothe, shelter and educate poor youngsters in 225 orphanages and shelters, 216 hospitals and clinics, 850 nurseries and 3,408 schools – of these 559 are vocational and technical, 91 agricultural, 1,440 high schools, 23 colleges,5 elementary schools.

The letter adds, "In all these various programs, the spirit and memory of St. John Bosco live on. The men and women who have followed in the footsteps have dedicated their lives to be friends, counselors, and educators of poor young people." The letter ends thus: (I did not see it at first; the Good Lord pointed it out to me):

"Not just caring for the poor children of the world but also teaching them to care for themselves."

At the right hand corner was a world map with the Cross of Jesus standing erect in the middle.

Here is another interesting message concerning this piece of writing that had been on my mind though Our Lord had already given me the answer. I was saying to myself I wonder if the audience would think I was being too bold in saying the Trinity and I are one.

As I sat in the office at Christ the King waiting to see someone, I picked up a Lenten booklet to read. And I saw what I already knew as the answer to the matter in question. I had remarked to a friend that the miraculous pictures in my books testify to my oneness with the Holy Trinity. In the Lenten booklet, I read something very interesting entitled the WORD among us edited by Leo Zanchettin. Jesus put my mind at ease again after reading what St. Athanasius, one of the African saints said concerning people like me. "We can be "Divinized," says St. Athanasius. He goes on to say that as far as the Church Fathers are concerned, "This promise of being filled with God's own life was at the heart of the Gospel message." Zanchettin says that no one was more emphatic on this subject than St. Athanasius, bishop of Alexandria, Egypt, who lived in the third century. In his treatise on the Incarnation, he wrote that God became man so that man might become God. He further explained that "God has divinized us by uniting us with Christ in baptism." Just as Christ took on our human nature, so it is God's plan that we humans also take on Christ's divine nature. St. Irenaeus of Lyon c. 125 agrees with St. Athanasius in these words, "The Glory of God is a living person and the life of a person consists in beholding God." According to St. Athanasius, Adam and Eve experienced direct intimacy with God in the Garden of Eden. Each day they were sharing God's life as they experienced His blessings which resulted in their being more and more like Him. The Holy Spirit can transform us whereby we begin to think, act and love just like Jesus. (I have experienced this life before; that is why I wrote on one of my pictures in my book *Divine Intimacy with my Saviour* that I once lived in heaven). But all that changed for Adam and Eve, and for us, too, when our first parents disobeyed God. What a pity!

St. Athanasius remarked that divinizaton is impossible without God's grace and power.

The saint remarked that no one could change what was corrupted into incorruptible, except the Saviour Himself.

On the Feast of All Saints, which was November 1st., I brought the picture of the Holy Trinity to where I was typing and I said, "Let us hear what Our Heavenly Father has to say concerning St. Athanasius' Treatise on the Incarnation. Immediately, the Holy Spirit booklet by Fr. Paul O'Sullivan caught my attention. When I opened it the first name I saw was St. Basil the Great, a great Saint indeed; so are all the Saints. I encourage everyone to read about the lives of the Saints. The following is what he has to say, "By the Holy Spirit each of the Saints is made divine as God Himself has declared, 'I have said you are gods.'" (St. Basil, Con Eunom.). His fellow Saints say the same thing. As I was getting ready to type this message, I kept running into a piece of old writing dated February, 1982 which, I thought was rather in my way. Before typing the above, I decided to look at it, and to my amazement, I see it has bearing on what I am writing. It states that, "Every Christian in a state of grace is another Christ."

Pastor Daniel explains his stance,

"For we are unto God a sweet savour of Christ" (11 Cor. 2:15) We are a sweet savour before God. If we are sweet savour before God, then there should be something very attractive about us. We are losing out in that quality of being spiritually attractive. The good pastor asks, "Why be repulsive'? Why be loathsome? Why be a contradictory as we show one thing outside but are something else inside? Why give a false signal around us?"

The pastor feels that one cannot expect a true Christian to live with such hypocrisy. He believes, "There should be repentance in us preachers first." He adds that he has always maintained that if a preacher is right the people are also right. He continues to say, "If there is a prophetic word from the Lord, then sin will be unmasked. "The sources of darkness will be quickly identified and dealt with." But he thinks that, "When a preacher is without prayer and when there is no prophetic light then you know you can have a very deathly and dark situation." He believes, "This is the present condition around the globe," and that the preachers, "are actually destroying the world through lack of revival, lack of power in prayer, and lack of credibility in the pulpit." He asks the question, "Why should we say we are Christians if our light does not shine that men will see our good works and glorify our Heavenly Father." If we are true Christians, it will be known, because, as Pastor Daniel says, light is seen, light illuminates, light enlightens the dark corners and that people want light around them. He asks fellow Christians if they are a source of light; that, whether they are able to pray till there is light? Also, whether, they are creating or emanating light? He further asks, "Are we illuminating every dark corner?" He laments, "Oh, it is so sad that even in Christian work people love comfort, ease and to have a little niche for themselves. And as they enlarge that niche and grow in self-satisfaction and in other comforts, they feel they have arrived." Pastor Daniel says, "What a curse to be those that get easily satisfied with one's own comfort". He repeats, "What a curse!" He asks whether, we are called to seek and design our own comfort. He continues, "Oh, to be a source of light in this dark World! Oh, to be an example to others. Oh, to be an inspiration to those who are crying to be inspired!"

He concludes by saying, "We have got to lay hold of Christ, that we have to repent of all these sources of darkness which we have permitted to permeate us; and that finally, we have got to be faithful to God." I then saw in the right hand corner of the pamphlet the following in big bold writing:

"THEN SPAKE JESUS

AGAIN UNTO THEM,

SAYING, I AM THE LIGHT

OF THE WORLD: HE THAT

FOLLOWS ME SHALL

NOT WALK IN DARKNESS

BUT SHALL HAVE THE

LIGHT OF LIFE"

JOHN 8:12

The last thing the Lord showed me was the Easter Candle with symbols of the Resurrection such as "I am the Alpha and the Omega" and, "He is Risen". Alleluia!"

Jesus is consecrating the Bread and the Wine to change into His own Body and Blood.
See the miracle of His Face under the Bread

This picture comes from The Shepherd's Voice - Most Holy Trinity Church, Detroit

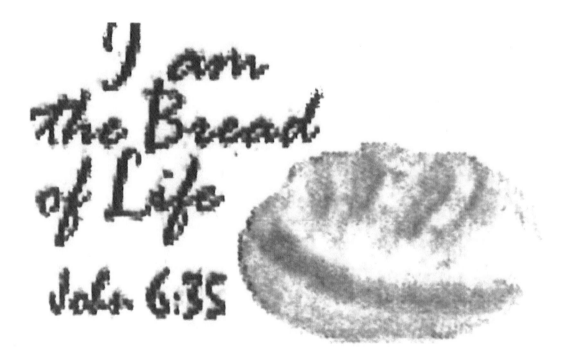

I am the Bread of Life

John 6:35

DO THIS IN REMEMBRANCE OF ME

The Lord had the H. Communion on His tongue.
A few days later on the Feast of I.H.M, amazingly
I found myself at Old St. Mary's for Mass,
and saw they received Holy Communion on the
tongue just as Jesus showed me.

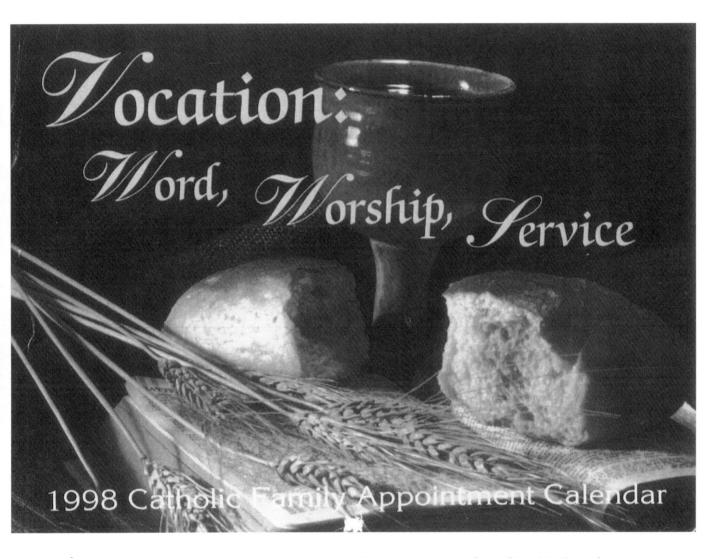

Christ's Face on the Eucharistic or Communion Bread. Picture was taken from Church Bulletin from Mission Santa Barbara, Santa Barbara, California

31

St. Clare is noted for her love for the Eucharist and is seen here carrying the Host

Look

THE EUCHARISTIC MIRACLE
"The Host changed into Flesh the Wine into Blood"
LANCIANO

PRAYER

O Jesus, living Bread descended from heaven, how infinitely great and good is Your love!

In order to perpetuate and strengthen our faith in Your Real Presence in the Eucharist, you changed the consecrated species of bread and wine into Flesh and Blood, which are perpetually reserved in the Eucharistic Sanctuary of Lanciano. Oh, increase ever more our faith in You, Sacramental Lord.

Grant that burning with love for You, we may come to seek comfort in dangers, in necessities and in anxieties, only at your feet, O Divine Prisoner of our tabernacles, O perpetual fount of every grace.

Excite in us hunger and thirst for Your Eucharistic food, so that in keeping Your Word, tasting this heavenly Bread, we may be able to enjoy true life now and forever. Amen.

3 Pater, Ave, Gloria.

Jesus appeared above Advent Wreath in the
image of the Holy Shroud on Christmas Eve, 2006.

Most Holy Redeemer Catholic Church

Adelaide

Most Holy Redeemer Catholic Church

Most Holy Redeemer Catholic Church

Adelaide

An emblem (IXOYE) having a mythical connection with Jesus,
being the first letters of the Greek words meaning Jesus Christ, God's
Son, Saviour. [Greek ichthys meaning fish]. This symbol was used by
Christians during the persecution. The emblem appeared miraculously
above the infant Jesus at Christmas (2009).

The flowers at Christmas exhibit the face of the Divine Child.

I took this picture of St. Joseph and the baby Jesus and the Virgin Mary appeared on the column—and our Lord Jesus too appeared.

John the Baptist on the River Jordan

John the Baptist raises up his finger bearing *Live Jesus* "The Lamb of God"

Live face of John the baptist.

John the Baptist and the Lamb

Photo by Mr. Shepherd, St. Anne, Windsor

Miraculous Head of Jesus crucified appeared
at Most Holy Redeemer – Christmas 2010

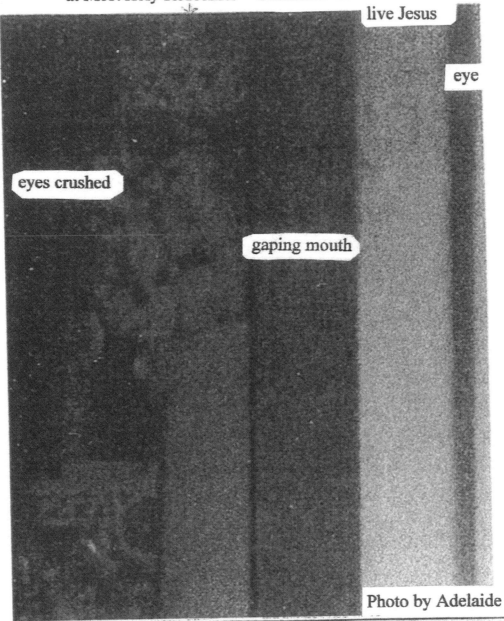

live Jesus

eye

eyes crushed

gaping mouth

Photo by Adelaide

**We adore you, Oh Christ, and we praise you.
By your Holy Cross you have redeemed the world.**

God so loved the world that
He gave His only Son, that whoever
believes in Him should not perish
but have eternal life.

John 3:16

JESUS WITH THE CROWN OF THORNS FROM THE HOLY SHROUD
as reconstructed by Cardinal Ricci

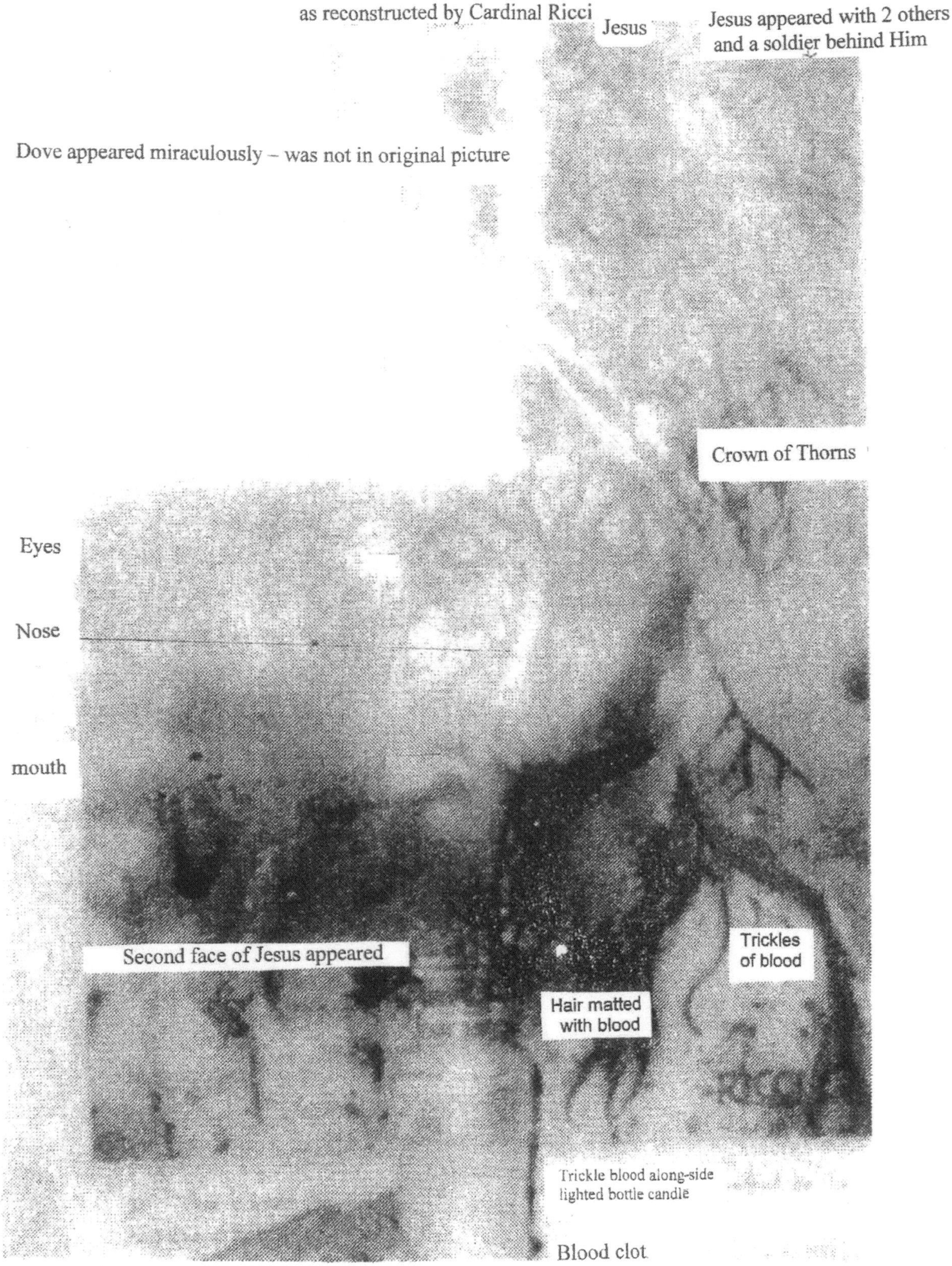

Jesus

Jesus appeared with 2 others
and a soldier behind Him

Dove appeared miraculously – was not in original picture

Crown of Thorns

Eyes

Nose

mouth

Second face of Jesus appeared

Trickles
of blood

Hair matted
with blood

Trickle blood along-side
lighted bottle candle

Blood clot

"For God so loved the world that He gave His only begotten Son, that whosoever believe in Him, may not perish, but have eternal life."   John 3:16 .

The public veneration of the Holy Cross originated in the Fourth century with the miraculous finding of the True Cross on September 14,326 by St. Helena, the mother of Roman emperor, Constantine, during a pilgrimage to Jerusalem. St. Helena found the Holy Cross on the same day that two churches built at the site of Calvary by her son were being dedicated. Constantine then built the Church of the Holy Sepulcher at the site of discovery. The Church was consecrated on September 13, and the Holy Cross was brought outside the church on September 14, for veneration by the clergy and the faithful. The observance of the Triumph of the Cross could be marked as that of Good Friday.

THE EXALTATION OF THE HOLY CROSS
Feast Day
September 14th

Adoramus te, Christe, et benedicimus tibi,
Quia per crucem tuam redemisti mundum.

We adore thee, O Christ, and we bless thee,

because by Thy Holy Cross Thou has redeemed the world!

Face of Jesus

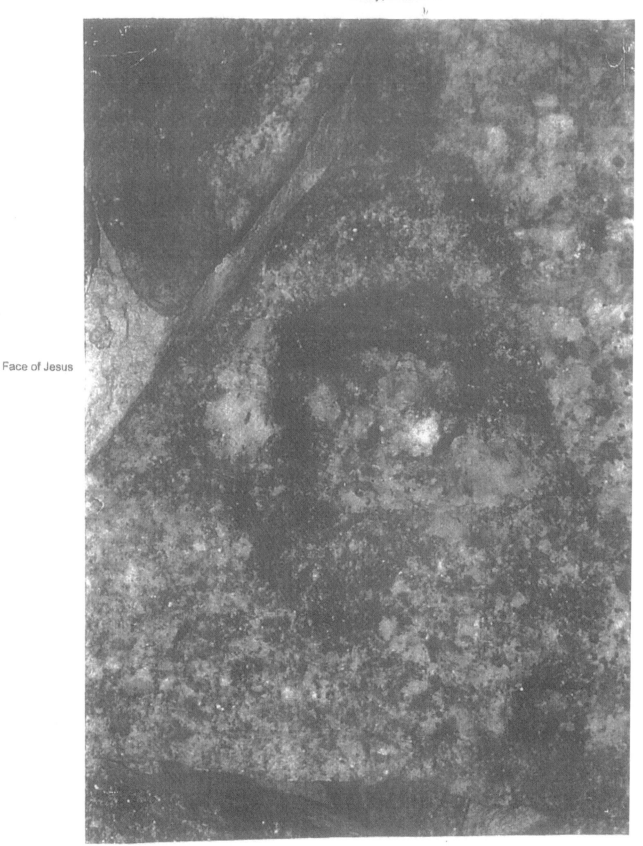

Jesus appeared at the grotto at St. Margaret Mary's Church with His mother behind Him in 2005, in Ghana

The Holy Face of Jesus

(After the Holy Shroud of Turin)

"By offering My Face to My Eternal Father,
nothing will be refused, and the conversion
of many sinners will be obtained."
—Our Lord
To Sr. Mary of St. Peter

"Rejoice, My Daughter, because the hour approaches when the most beautiful work under the sun will be born."
—Our Lord
To Sister Mary of St. Peter

The Holy Face of Jesus
from the image on Veronica's veil.
(The veil is kept in St. Peter's Basilica, Rome.)

Immaculate Heart of Mary Picture. I saw a 2nd. Hello being drawn
around her head

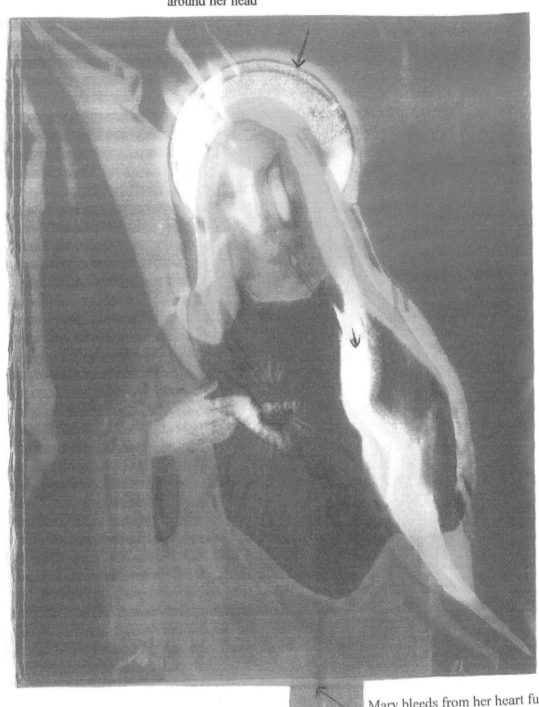

I saw a difference in the picture the same day I

heard about the Apparition of the Holy Shroud in Ghana.

Mary bleeds from her heart fulfilling
Simeon's prophecy—(and a sword will
pierce through your soul). Lk. 2:35

FACE OF JESUS
from the Holy Shroud of Turin

Pietà (part.) · Città del Vaticano, Basilica di San Pietro

I brought this Pieta Picture from the Vatican and Mary is crying
(Nov.23, 2008)

The Holy Spirit descended upon me in the company of the Holy Trinity on the Feast of Corpus Christi - 2006

Jesus' Face appeared on the back of my hand where you see a ray of light at
Most Holy Redeemer on Good Friday

This picture was taken at St. Joseph's Shrine where we found the Exhibition of the Holy Shroud

Jesus

This picture was taken as we walked our way through the Via Dolorosa following
the route Jesus took to Calvary. I see a crying lamb at my feet & Jesus' face on
the envelope with prayer request and my Prayer Book

Miracle of Jesus & His Mother at the grotto
small Cross(palm)

Profile of Jesus appeared
after I placed a small
palm branch woven into
a Cross

Arm of Jesus holding
a Lamb & Letter "V"

Lamb

Jesus reclined on my cheek and chest when I visited Him on Palm
Sunday at the grotto in Ghana where He had appeared. Our Lord was
holding a 'Lamb' and the 'Letter V'

Miracle at St. M.Mary
of Jesus and His mother
behind Him

Adelaide

——(small green palm branch)
_Second face of Jesus appeared
after placing the small palm

WHO HAS BELIEVEDWHAT WE HAVE HEARD
AND TO WHOM HAS THE ARM OF THE LORD
    BEEN REVEALED?
FOR HE GREW UP BEFORE HIM LIKE A
          YOUNG PLANT
AND LIKE A ROOT OUT OF THE DRY GROUND
HE HAD NO FORM OR COMELINESS THAT WE
     SHOULD LOOK AT HIM
AND NO BEAUTY THAT WE SHOULD DESIRE HIM.
HE WAS DESPISED AND REJECTED BY MEN;
A MAN OF SORROWS, AND ACQUAINTED WITH GRIEF;
AND AS ONE FROM WHOM MEN HIDE THEIR FACES
HE WAS DESPISED, AND WE ESTEEMED HIM NOT.
SURELY HE HAS BORNE OUR GRIEFS AND CARRIED
     OUR SORROWS; ETC.

                    Isaiah   53

Jesus and Adelaide in arms at the grotto in Accra, Ghana

The Lord used my teenage picture to show me what happened when one of the soldiers pierced His side. I saw the blood rising and filling my chest from one side to the other. There was so much blood I coul1d not bear to watch. When I came back I noticed the blood had gone back but the lower part by the black belt was tainted with blood and I could see His face all over the top part of my outfit and the place where I had my hand crossed.

My teenage picture when I lived in Heaven

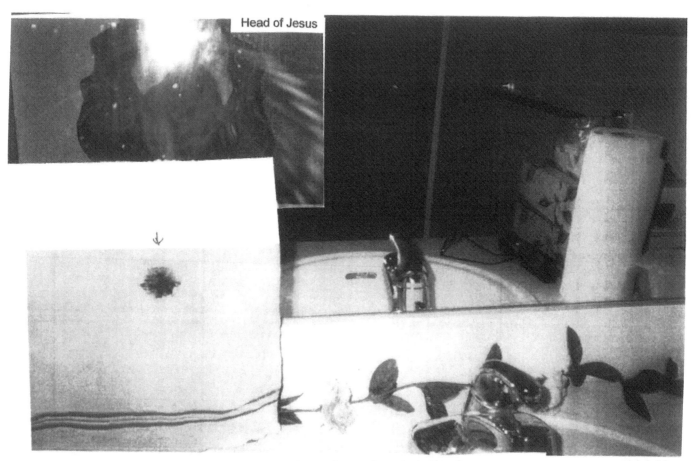

Head of Jesus

Jesus advises me to observe Lent pressing my hand on my face towel to make the sign of the Cross

Adelaide

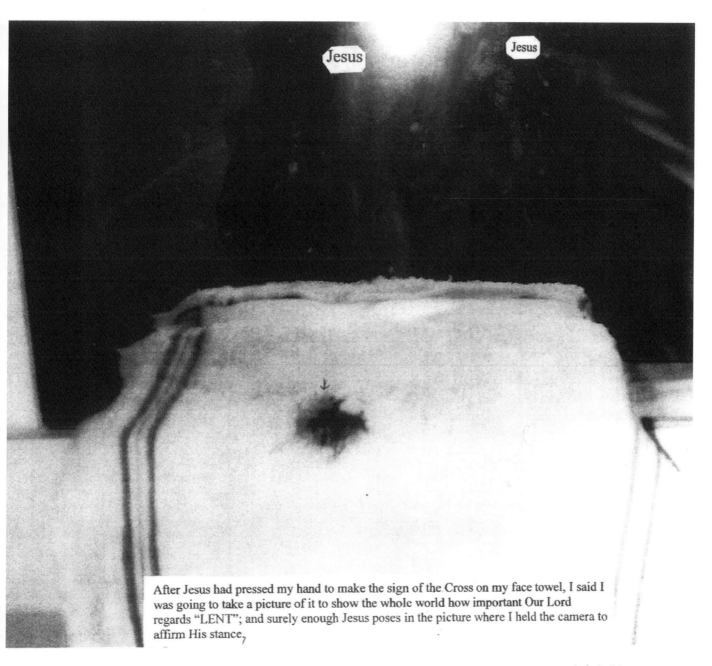

After Jesus had pressed my hand to make the sign of the Cross on my face towel, I said I was going to take a picture of it to show the whole world how important Our Lord regards "LENT"; and surely enough Jesus poses in the picture where I held the camera to affirm His stance.

Adelaide

This is the Holy Cross I used for Evangelization at St. Joseph's Shrine in Santa Cruz.
See all the light emanating from the Holy Cross. Look at my both hands. Jesus still bleeds
for our sins. Christ has His Head on each of my left fingers. My feet are saturated with blood
signifying the Lord's Crucifixion.

Picture was taken at Immaculate Heart of Mary now Corpus Christi Church, Detroit

"From Thy side, pierced with a lance by a soldier, blood and water issued forth until there was not left in Thy Body a single drop; and finally, like a bundle of myrrh lifted to the top of the Cross, Thy delicate flesh was destroyed, the very substance of Thy Body withered, and the Marrow of Thy Bones dried."

From The Pieta Prayer Book

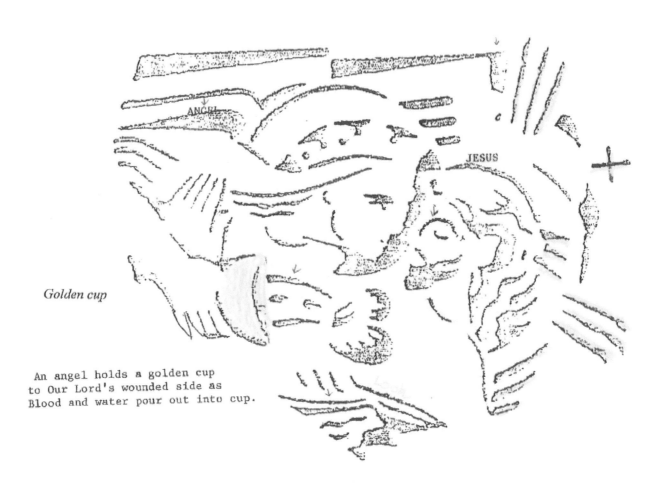

Golden cup

An angel holds a golden cup
to Our Lord's wounded side as
Blood and water pour out into cup.

My fingers are saturated with blood because of Christ's head on the leaf

The Holy Spirit descended upon me in the company of the Holy Trinity
on the Feast of Corpus Christi – 2006

Adelaide

This picture was taken at St. Joseph's Shrine where we had the Holy Shroud Exhibition

A miracle- the Shroud of Turin

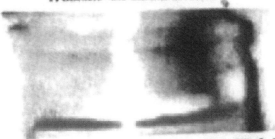

Jesus' Face appears on the bottle candle during Holy Week April (2010)

This picture was taken at Corpus Christi College, Oxford, England.

The symbol for Corpus Christi or the Eucharist is the pelican feeding its young from her own blood

Christ kisses my feet as He did His apostles on Holy Thursday during The Last Supper

My yellow jacket turned bloody because of Our Blessed Saviour's Head on the Jacket
and at the back of my hand

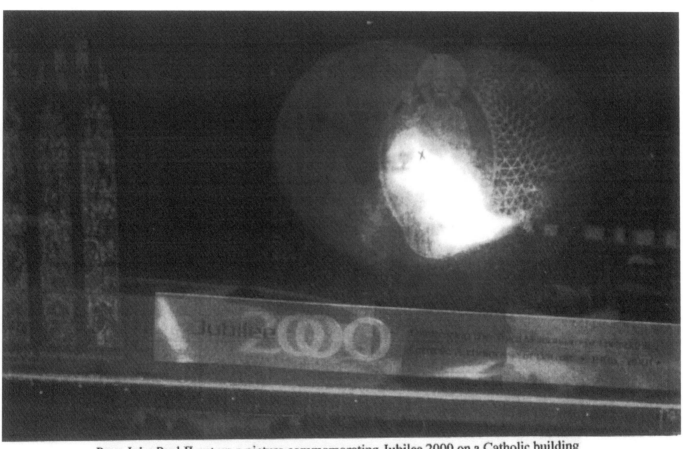

Pope John Paul II put up a picture commemorating Jubilee 2000 on a Catholic building down town, and when I took a picture of it, the Cup of Salvation showed up; along with it was the picture of the Last Supper.

Adelaide

This Last Supper Picture was taken downtown

Resurrection of Jesus — April 16, 2006

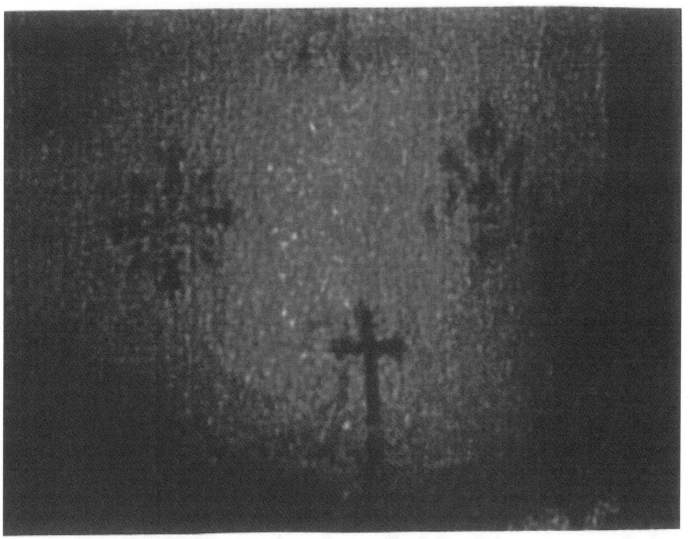

This picture was taken at St. Anne Church, Detroit   Joe Lee

Jesus appeared on April 16, 2006 at St. Anne's Catholic Church – Detroit

This picture shows the risen Lord in yellow apparel.

Jesus appeared on my shawl. Picture was taken at Immaculate Heart of Mary
with two lovely communicants on Easter Sunday

Easter Sunday – The Risen Lord appeared on my shawl

The Risen Lord

Christ appeared again on Easter Sunday 2010 at Ste Anne Catholic Church – Detroit

Jesus appeared on both sides of red-marked Cross on top of Easter Candle

The Risen Lord

A miracle of the Holy Spirit
at the Lord's feet

Adelaide

Jesus in the Tabernacle at St. Thomas, the apostle, to whom Christ said after His Resurrection, "Have you come to believe because you have seen me? Blessed are those who have not seen and yet believe.   John 20:26-29

Jesus appeared again on Easter Sunday April 12. 2009 at St. Anne Catholic Church

The Risen Christ at my finger tips

Jesus glides through the clouds from heaven to meet St. Margaret Mary
at the Convent of Visitation

Adelaide

(from the Vatican)

A miracle of the Risen Lord with the Head tossed backwards

Joe Lee

Jesus appeared again on Easter Sunday March 23, 2008.

I was looking for a picture of the Holy Family when they brought Jesus to Simeon in the temple and a letter came in the mail with a stamp of the picture I was looking for.

School Year picture- The Good Lord was with me throughout my Teaching Center

Ascension of Jesus

Jesus left His Foot imprint on Mt. of Olives as He ascended into heaven.

Jesus appeared over my head and on my arm during the Feast Day of His Grandma St. Anne, July 26, 2010. My arm is resting on St. Anne's thigh.

Jesus

Jesus by His own tabernacle

THE RISEN LORD

"Look beyond the Bread you eat, look beyond the Wine you drink."
Rejoice and be glad for The Lord has risen indeed.
ALLELUIA